CLICK, CLACK, MOO
Cows That Type

For my Dad —D.C.
To Sue Dooley —B.L.

ARTIST'S NOTE:

For this book I did brush drawings using Windsor Newton lamp black watercolor on tracing paper. I then had the drawings photocopied onto one-ply Strathmore kid finish watercolor paper and applied watercolor washes to the black drawings. The advantage to this method is that I can get as many copies on the watercolor paper as I want, and I can experiment with the color, choosing the finishes that I like the best.

SIMON & SCHUSTER BOOKS FOR YOUNG READERS An imprint of Simon & Schuster Children's Publishing Division, 1230 Avenue of the Americas New York, NY 10020. Text copyright © 2000 by Doreen Cronin. Illustrations copyright © 2000 by Betsy Lewin. Cover illustrations copyright © 2000 Betsy Lewin. Original jacket design by Anahid Hamparian. Paper cover adapted by Center for the Collaborative Classroom. All right reserved including the right of reproduction in whole or in part in any form. SIMON & SCHUSTER BOOKS FOR YOUNG READERS is a trademark of Simon & Schuster Book design by Anahid Hamparian. The text of this book is set in 30 point Filosofia Bold.

This Center for the Collaborative Classroom edition is reprinted by arrangement with Atheneum Books for Young Readers, an imprint of Simon & Schuster Children's Publishing Division.

Center for the Collaborative Classroom
1001 Marina Village Parkway, Suite 110
Alameda, CA 94501
800.666.7270 * fax: 510.464.3670
collaborativeclassroom.org

ISBN 978-1-61003-342-8
Printed in China

7 8 9 10 RRD 20 19

CLICK, CLACK, MOO
Cows That Type

by Doreen Cronin   pictures by Betsy Lewin

Center for the Collaborative Classroom

Farmer Brown has a problem.
His cows like to type.
All day long he hears

Click, clack, **moo.**
　　Click, clack, **moo.**
Clickety, clack, **moo.**

At first, he couldn't believe his ea[r]
Cows that type?
Impossible!

Click, clack, **moo.**
 Click, clack, **moo.**
Clickety, clack, **moo.**

Then, he couldn't believe his eyes.

Dear Farmer Brown,
The barn is very cold
at night.
We'd like some electric
blankets.
Sincerely,
The Cows

It was bad enough the cows had found the old typewriter in the barn, now they wanted electric blankets! "No way," said Farmer Brown. "No electric blankets."

So the cows went on strike. They left a note on the barn door.

Sorry.
We're closed.
No milk
today.

"No milk today!" cried Farmer Brown. In the background, he heard the cows busy at work:

Click, clack, **moo.**
Click, clack, **moo.**
Clickety, clack, **moo.**

The next day, he got another note:

Dear Farmer Brown,
The hens are cold too.
They'd like electric
blankets.
Sincerely,
The Cows

The cows were growing impatient with the farmer. They left a new note on the barn door.

No eggs!" cried Farmer Brown.
the background he heard
nem.

lick, clack, **moo.**
Click, clack, **moo.**
lickety, clack, **moo.**

"Cows that type. Hens on strike! Whoever heard of such a thing? How can I run a farm with no milk and no eggs!" Farmer Brown was furious.

Farmer Brown got out his own typewriter.

Dear Cows and Hens:
There will be no electric blankets.
You are cows and hens.
I demand milk and eggs.
Sincerely,
Farmer Brown

Duck was a neutral party, so he brought the ultimatum to the cows.

The cows held an emergency meeting. All the animals gathered around the barn to snoop, but none of them could understand Moo.

All night long, Farmer Brown waited for an answer.

Duck knocked on the door early
the next morning. He handed
Farmer Brown a note:

Dear Farmer Brown,

We will exchange our typewriter for electric blankets.

Leave them outside the barn door and we will send Duck over with the typewriter.

Sincerely,
The Cows

Farmer Brown decided this was
a good deal. He left the blankets